LARRY ULRICH

Four Corners region

THE ANCESTRAL PUEBLOAN WAY

The roots of the ancestral Puebloans are not entirely clear. Archeologists have found plenty of cultural artifacts showing that foragers lived in the Southwest between 8,000 and 2,000 years ago, and definitive evidence that big game hunters lived here before that. Archeologists call the people with the foraging economy "Archaic" or "Desert Culture." These people realized their strength and survival lay in flexibility. They subsisted on plants as well as animals, a response to the increased aridity that accompanied the end of the glacial period.

Highly mobile, these nomads moved where food and water took them, expanding their range and exploiting every nook and cranny of the environment. They carried only lightweight tool kits and throwing sticks to extend the range of their spears. Traveling in small family groups of perhaps three to eight people, they settled down just long enough to build crude huts and "sleeping circles." Their passage is marked mainly by the debris of stone chips left from their toolmaking.

The ancestral Puebloan people may have grown out of a northern branch of these Archaic people, or

Prehistoric corncobs

they may have been homesteaders of a culture who came to the Four Corners area from the south. In any case, around 2,000 years ago the first discernible stage of ancestral Puebloan culture emerged. Their presence is marked in the archeological record by semi-permanent or permanent dwellings and evidence of domesticated plant cultivation, including digging sticks, grinding stones, and storage rooms.

They were called the "Basket People" by Mancos, Colorado, rancher Richard Wetherill. An amateur archeologist, Wetherill had excavated and collected remains in the dry caves of Grand Gulch in southeast Utah during the winters in the 1890s. There he found fine basketry, woven matting and cord, and stone tools and digging sticks—the hallmarks of these earliest ancestral Puebloans. Wetherill insightfully distinguished the makers of these items from the cliff dwellers he had identified at Mesa Verde.

The primary domesticated plant grown by these Basketmakers was maize, better known as corn. Corn evolved from a wild grass called *teosinte,* which grows in Mexico. Researchers have found an early variety of corn, about seven thousand years old, preserved in caves in Mexico. People brought the seeds, along with the knowledge of how to grow corn, from Mexico by way of southern and central New Mexico. Attentive farmers crossbred and selected the strongest seeds and cached them for the following year's crop. Eventually types of corn resulted that could survive the colder climate and shorter growing season of the Four Corners.

In northern Arizona the earliest variety was probably a popcorn, with twelve or fourteen rows of small kernels on small cobs. As time passed, an eight-rowed flour corn gained favor. Fewer rows meant bigger kernels and more nutrition from a single kernel.

MICHAEL COLLIER

Squash, also from Mexico, was grown alongside corn. The hardened shells of these gourd-type squash made handy water jugs, and the seeds were edible as well.

Ancestral Puebloan gardeners mostly dry-farmed, timing their planting to take advantage of the life-giving moisture of spring snowmelt and summer rains. This was an especially risky operation in the Southwest, given the predictably unpredictable weather.

Fields often were planted in sand dunes or placed at the mouth of an arroyo or near a spring. Farmers broke ground with a stone hoe and poked a hole about a foot deep with a wooden digging stick. Uttering the proper prayers, they gently placed corn seeds into the hole, where they could germinate in the moisture held by the sandy soil.

In July, as he surveyed the progress of the small bushy corn plants, his eyes turned to the sky, beseeching the towering clouds to deliver rain. In an attempt to help nature along, he might lay up rock terraces on hillsides and erect check dams across creeks to help channel water and collect soil. At Mesa Verde, the people built a half-million gallon reservoir. In Glen Canyon on the Utah-Arizona border, and elsewhere, archeologists have found

Granary at Grand Gulch, Utah

canal systems, indicating that ancestral Puebloan farmers dabbled a little with irrigation.

As important as agriculture became to these people, they did not forget how their ancestors managed to survive. When the harvest failed to materialize, they turned to an ages-old seasonal round, gathering wild plants and hunting animals. The delicious, calorie-rich nut of the piñon pine was a staple. In autumn, when the fat cones were bursting with seeds, entire families took to the woodlands. They shook the cones from the branches and collected them in baskets. They roasted the seeds on the spot or took them home to grind them into meal.

JACK DYKINGA

The generous fruit of the banana yucca provided a source of food, as did greens from pigweed and amaranth, members of the goosefoot family. Crimson fruit was plucked from the tops of prickly pear pads and dried in the sun, the sweet results to be savored later. The people never abandoned hunting either, for jackrabbits, prairie dogs, or mule deer provided hearty protein.

Though corn agriculture became a huge part of their lives, these Basketmakers did not completely

Agave and piñon cone

GEORGE H. H. HUEY

Reconstructed pit house, Mesa Verde National Park

settle down until about 1,500 years ago, when three major innovations—the bow and arrow, pottery, and permanent pithouse dwellings—revolutionized their way of life. At this time, the bow and arrow almost entirely replaced the spear and atlatl, or throwing stick, as the principal hunting weapon. The well-made, portable baskets used for storing water and cooking food were largely supplanted by more durable and less perishable pottery. These technological changes coincided with a more settled existence for the ancestral Puebloans.

With pottery came the introduction of a third crop—beans—uniting with corn and squash to form an almost sacred agricultural trinity in the pre-Columbian Southwest. The common bean *(Phaseolus vulgaris)*, along with kidney and navy beans, were among the nutritious legumes grown by the ancestral Puebloans.

The ancestral Puebloans became bound to the soil and to rain and preoccupied with storing any surplus food. Ears of corn were stacked up like cords of wood,

and a full larder no doubt marked a measure of wealth among the ancestral Puebloans.

The change to a stable, sedentary farming life also involved construction of permanent houses. The first ones were simple brush-and-pole structures built over pits dug into the ground. Several were built together to form small villages. Later, people constructed above-ground masonry towns in an architectural evolution that is a major feature of ancestral Puebloan culture.

STICKS AND STONES

Accommodation. In all aspects of their lives—but especially regarding their homes—this word best describes the ancestral Puebloans. Throughout the thousand years that their culture flourished, they built according to the dictates of the land. At its height, their finest architecture exhibited an extraordinary and harmonious blending with their land of rock.

The earliest homes were simple, nothing more than single pits dug a few feet into the ground. Walls were lined with rock slabs, and pole roofs were covered with brush and mud. The ancestral Puebloan adoption of pit-house architecture indicates that they had determined it was worth their while to invest labor even in these crude structures. Imagine a family sneaking a look at their neighbor's endeavors, and holding lengthy discussions on the best materials and solutions to vexing local problems. Friends may have shared information about a labor-saving digging tool, the location of the best roofing material, or the source of an especially workable rock.

Puebloan pithouses were circular, square, rectangular, or D-shaped in plan. Four hefty upright posts were crossed with ceiling joists, then overlaid with a lattice of slender poles, brush, and grass or bark matting. An earthen covering provided extra protection and insulation from the elements. A central hearth in the floor served

Prehistoric arrows

both for cooking and heating, and smoke was ventilated through a side shaft and a smoke hole in the roof. Where water and soil were available, loose-knit communities of pithouses inevitably developed, especially as the importance of agriculture to the economy increased.

More than one observer has reflected on conditions in these close quarters: cold, dark, smoky, sometimes damp, with the smell of debris attracting insects. Yet despite these conditions, in this embryonic stage grew the seed of ancestral Puebloan evolution.

By 1,300 years ago a significant architectural shift occurred. In many areas—but not all—subterranean homes were being replaced by aboveground structures. Rocks were laid up in courses to make walled rooms. Several rooms were then connected into rectangular blocks, and second and third stories were added to create a honeycomb of rooms. The ancestral Puebloans nearly always oriented their pueblos to the south to take advantage of the warming sun.

The masons must have taken great pride in their work. Fine rock shaping and meticulous mortar work is evident in many buildings. Walls consisted of a core of rubble faced with a veneer of shaped stone blocks, or they were single or double courses of large sandstone blocks. If the builder was in a hurry for a home, he would use *jacal* (hah-CALL) construction, an interweaving of mud and sticks. Poles, overlaid with woven splints of willow, rush, or juniper and a final layer of mud, repeated the pithouse roofing technique.

Curiously, the excellent masonry often was plastered entirely with mud, inside and out, and sometimes painted with a whitewash. Small doorways were characteristic of masonry dwellings, and the T-shape was distinctively ancestral Puebloan. Why the T-shape no one really knows. Perhaps burdens could be carried into a room more easily, or a blanket may have been hung over half the doorway.

For nearly five centuries masonry pueblo architecture was the standard dwelling form, seen in thousands of ruins throughout the Four Corners region. The three major centers of ancestral Puebloan culture each exhibit a distinctive masonry style: Chaco, the finest; Mesa Verde, the best known; and Kayenta, the least carefully executed. In the more rugged Kayenta area, pithouses persisted into the thirteenth century, alongside striking

GEORGE H. H. HUEY

pueblo dwellings such as Betatakin and Keet Seel. Beyond masonry living structures, the people of the northern San Juan–Mesa Verde area also built round, square, and D-shaped towers several stories high that might have served communication or astronomical functions. Some of the most elegant examples of these towers still stand at Hovenweep on the Colorado-Utah border.

Pueblos usually embraced a plaza with a special type of pithouse—a kiva—in the center. In modern pueblos, the most sacred ceremonies are held in kivas. Ancestral Puebloan kivas usually included a bench where

Spruce Tree House, Mesa Verde National Park

TOM TILL

*Pueblo Bonito, Chaco Culture National
Historical Park*

people could sit, and a particular hole in the floor known as a *sipapu*. In many Pueblo origin stories, the sipapu is the hole through which the people emerged from the subterranean third world into the fourth and final world in which they now live.

Kivas were the community and ceremonial centers of the ancestral Puebloan world. The people used the kivas for prayer, initiation into religious societies, and the veneration of their ancestors. Ceremonies related to planting, harvesting, and the annual calendar would begin in the kivas. The warmth of the rooms in winter provided a comfortable space for storytelling, weaving, socializing, gaming, and discussing pressing community issues.

At the traditional time of year, sometimes on a frigid winter night, dark figures disappeared down ladders into the confines of the kiva. Glowing sparks flew from the smoke hole, and the smell of juniper filled the air. Villagers moved purposefully about the plazas, making careful preparations. At some mysterious signal, as many people as possible filled the plazas and waited patiently for the dancers. They appeared from the kivas, dressed in deer hide leggings, faces painted or covered with masks. Their trancelike chants, accompanied by the sound of turtle rattles and drumming, lasted through the night until everyone was exhausted.

At a few places the ancestral Puebloans erected very large kivas. At Aztec Ruins in northern New Mexico archeologist Earl Morris excavated an example of such a specialized kiva. Under the auspices of the American Museum of Natural History, Morris reconstructed and reroofed one of these so-called "great kivas." At Aztec, Chaco, Mesa Verde, and elsewhere, these circular kivas, some as large as sixty feet in diameter, are believed to have acted as centers where people from outlying areas gathered with their counterparts in the larger communities to participate in ceremonies and celebrations.

Aztec also contains a curious feature known as a tri-wall structure. As the name implies, these were unusual buildings of three concentric walls that also may have been used for ceremonies.

FRED HIRSCHMANN

Architecture is important not only for what it says about a people's lifestyle, but also for what it conveys about social organization and population. For example, the way room walls adjoin can suggest possible kinship ties. For the ancestral Puebloans, the evolution of architecture shows that society evolved from small hamlet, to village, to town. Development seems to have reached a peak at the site of Yellow Jacket near Cortez, Colorado, the largest single prehistoric town now known in the Four Corners region. Here more than eighteen hundred rooms arranged along streets are believed to have housed nearly three thousand people.

Timber beams used in dwellings have provided southwestern archeologists with their most important resource for dating ruins. Annual growth rings in the wood furnish the vital information. Trees, especially pines, add a ring each year, with wider rings in moist

Chacoan masonry

years and thinner ones in drought years. Scientists compare the rings in beams from ancestral Puebloan sites to a master chronology that extends into prehistoric times. Tree-ring dating is so valuable because it furnishes absolute rather than relative dates. The results can be cross-referenced with another artifact of singular importance to archeology—pottery.

COILS OF CLAY

The origin of pottery among the ancestral Puebloans is as murky as the origin of the culture itself. Pottery may have been a local discovery, as simple as someone noticing that they could mold mud in the bottom of a basket for better seed parching. On some early pots, basket stitch marks can be seen on the outside, suggesting that baskets were used for support during shaping.

Pottery also may have been imported from the Mogollon area to the south, either by traders or emigrants. The ancestral Puebloans liked what they saw and immediately began to make their own pots. In fact, the earliest pottery known from the ancestral Puebloan area is a brownware that looks very much like the pottery found in the Mogollon area, lending credence to the importation idea.

The impetus for adopting pottery may have been domestication of beans. Because of their long cooking time, beans demanded a vessel sturdier than a basket. Because pottery is not nearly as portable as lightweight baskets, its presence signals to us that people had settled into a sedentary existence. Other advantages of pottery over basketry were ease of manufacture, suitability for storing food securely, and resistance to fire and water.

As a tool for archeologists, pottery is indispensible: They can analyze potsherds, intact and plentiful at prehistoric sites, to date the sites and reveal changes in events, ideas, and trade interactions among people.

Tusayan corrugated jar

GEORGE H. H. HUEY

Potters require two basic ingredients—clay and temper (a substance that prevents cracking while a piece dries). People used what was locally available. When a potter found a prized source of clay, she would return to it again and again. The clays of the Four Corners region required firing in a reducing atmosphere (one without oxygen), producing a gray or white ware that distinguishes ancestral Puebloan pottery.

The ancestral Puebloans used a coil-and-scrape technique to build a pot. The clay was moistened until malleable enough to work. The potter next added temper, usually sand, although plant material, crushed rock, or even crushed potsherds were also used. The potter gently laid up coils of clay, one on top of another, pinching them together and scraping them smooth with a shell, gourd rind, or potsherd. A corrugated style, decorated with finger impressions on the outside, was the everyday cookware of the people. Pots could also be slipped with a wet clay glaze and polished to a smooth sheen.

Pueblo potters today believe that the vessels that hold their food or water possess life. Not surprisingly, they and their ancestors raised this significant craft to an art form. Early ancestral Puebloan gray ware developed into distinctive black-on-white ware, later followed by polychromes of more than two colors. Black-on-white pottery reached its heyday between 850 and 1250, about the same time that aboveground pueblos were replacing pithouses. Black paint was obtained from minerals or from plants like beeweed and was skillfully applied with a yucca brush. Red ocher was another valuable pigment, added to the outside of a vessel after firing to form what is called "fugitive red."

Early ancestral Puebloan potters adopted the same designs they had used in their basketry—geometric elements including lines and bands, triangles, scrolls, dots, and hachures. Potters combined these elements in an infinite number of ways, limited only by their imaginations.

Though devotion to geometry persisted, design elements, motifs, and symmetry became more sophisticated and ornate. Use of the same designs, paint, and temper became characteristic of certain regions in the Four Corners. As time went on, potters used their craft to make a statement, and individual styles emerge. At

GEORGE H. H. HUEY

one site a researcher studied the firing, polishing, shaping, and design of 250 pots and identified "signature" pots made by a total of twenty-six individual potters.

All kinds of ceramics were produced to serve various functions—jars, bowls, ollas, ladles, pitchers, mugs, seed jars, and even effigies and figurines, which may have held religious significance. Cooking jars can be recognized by their wide mouths and unsmoothed bands of clay around the neck. In the Mesa Verde area, strap handles were attached to the sides of water jugs for easier carrying. At Chaco, tall cylindrical jars were popular, and at Mesa Verde potters made a classic black-and-white mug.

Pottery also tells us that these were an amazingly mobile people who walked immense distances to trade and establish new settlements. Signs of this movement

Bandelier black-on-white bowl

are everywhere, in the abundance of traded pottery at sites and in the relatively brief time they lived in one place.

MOVEMENT

Pithouses were lived in, on average, only about fifteen years. Tree-ring studies show that even the largest pueblos, in which the ancestral Puebloans obviously invested considerable labor, were rarely occupied for more than about eighty years.

The same sites commonly were occupied, vacated, and reoccupied through time, as the people moved back and forth from lower to higher elevations, from creek bottoms to mesa tops to canyon heads. These local movements were almost certainly dictated by the vagaries of climate and the availability of water. During warmer, drier times the mesa tops proved farmable; when the climate grew cooler and wetter, lower elevations proved better. Though nature usually called the shots, people may also have been forced to move by actions of their own—depleting firewood, wearing out the soil, and over-harvesting plants and animals.

These local meanderings are matched by regional movements that have at their roots even more complex causes. A so-called "great drought" beginning around 1276 is most often cited as the reason many people moved away from the Four Corners area. But archeologists think now that the drought was not as severe or as far-reaching as originally believed. They puzzle over the different timings and patterns of peoples' movements from region to region.

The Chaco area in northwest New Mexico was the first to reach its golden years and the first that people left. The bustle of activity at Chaco Canyon started around 1,100 years ago. Irrigation systems, an extensive road network, and a dozen great houses were built in this desert valley. Construction boomed about 980 years ago.